SONG FOR A BIRTH OR A DEATH

ELIZABETH JENNINGS

Song for a Birth or a Death

and other poems

ANDRE DEUTSCH

FIRST PUBLISHED 1961 BY
ANDRE DEUTSCH LIMITED
105 GREAT RUSSELL STREET
LONDON WC I
COPYRIGHT © 1961 BY ELIZABETH JENNINGS
ALL RIGHTS RESERVED
PRINTED IN THE NETHERLANDS
BY DRUKKERIJ HOLLAND N.V.
AMSTERDAM

FOR S

Acknowledgements are due to the Editors of the following magazines and anthologies in which some of these poems first appeared:

The Cornhill, The Nation (USA), *New Statesman, The London Magazine, The Listener, Listen, The Times Literary Supplement, The Observer, The English Review of Literature, The Tablet, The PEN Anthologies 1960 & 1961, The Saturday Book 1960, The Aylesford Review, Gemini, Tomorrow, The Critical Quarterly, The Wind and the Rain,* also to the BBC Third Programme.

CONTENTS

Song for a Birth or a Death ▬   *Page* 13
Family Affairs   14
A Game of Chess   15
My Grandmother ▬   16
Passage from Childhood   17
In Praise of Creation   18
World I have Not Made   19
Harvest and Consecration   20
A World of Light   21
Notes for A Book of Hours I–IV   23
A Confession   27
A Requiem   28
At A Mass   29
John of the Cross   30
Catherine of Siena   31
The Resurrection   33
The Counterpart   34
Mantegna's *Agony in the Garden*   35
The Retreat   36
Visit to an Artist   37
The Clown I–VI   38
Lazarus   44
The Diamond Cutter   45
Stargazers and Others   46
To a Friend with a Religious Vocation   47
Children and Death   49
A Kind of Understanding   50
Visit to a Friend in Hospital   51
Greek Statues   52
The Pride of Life   53

CONTENTS

Men Fishing in the Arno	*Page*	54
An English Summer		55
The Room		56
Two Deaths		57
About These Things		58
No Reply		59
The Unfulfilled		60
No Child		61
The Instrument		62
Remembering Fireworks		63

SONG FOR A BIRTH OR A DEATH

SONG FOR A BIRTH OR A DEATH

Last night I saw the savage world
And heard the blood beat up the stair;
The fox's bark, the owl's shrewd pounce,
The crying creatures – all were there,
And men in bed with love and fear.

The slit moon only emphasised
How blood must flow and teeth must grip.
What does the calm light understand,
The light which draws the tide and ship
And drags the owl upon its prey
And human creatures lip to lip?

Last night I watched how pleasure must
Leap from disaster with its will:
The fox's fear, the watch-dog's lust
Know that all matings mean a kill:
And human creatures kissed in trust
Feel the blood throb to death until

The seed is struck, the pleasure's done,
The birds are thronging in the air;
The moon gives way to widespread sun.
Yes but the pain still crouches where
The young fox and the child are trapped
And cries of love are cries of fear.

FAMILY AFFAIRS

No longer here the blaze that we'd engender
Out of pure wrath. We pick at quarrels now
As fussy women stitch at cotton, slow
Now to forget and too far to surrender.
The anger stops, apologies also.

And in this end of summer, weighted calm
(Climate of mind, I mean), we are apart
Further than ever when we wished most harm.
Indifference lays a cold hand on the heart;
We need the violence to keep us warm.

Have we then learnt at last how to untie
The bond of birth, umbilical long cord,
So that we live quite unconnected by
The blood we share? What monstrous kind of sword
Can sever veins and still we do not die?

A GAME OF CHESS

The quiet moves, the gently shaded room:
It is like childhood once again when I
Sat with a tray of toys and you would come
To take my temperature and make me lie
Under the clothes and sleep. Now peacefully

We sit above the intellectual game.
Pure mathematics seems to rule the board
Emotionless. And yet I feel the same
As when I sat and played without a word
Inventing kingdoms where great feelings stirred.

Is it that knight and king and small squat castle
Store up emotion, bring it under rule,
So that the problems now with which we wrestle
Seem simply of the mind? Do feelings cool
Beneath the order of an abstract school?

Never entirely, since the whole thing brings
Me back to childhood when I was distressed:
You seem the same who put away my things
At night, my toys and tools of childish lust.
My king is caught now in a world of trust.

MY GRANDMOTHER

She kept an antique shop – or it kept her.
Among Apostle spoons and Bristol glass,
The faded silks, the heavy furniture,
She watched her own reflection in the brass
Salvers and silver bowls, as if to prove
Polish was all, there was no need of love.

And I remember how I once refused
To go out with her, since I was afraid.
It was perhaps a wish not to be used
Like antique objects. Though she never said
That she was hurt, I still could feel the guilt
Of that refusal, guessing how she felt.

Later, too frail to keep a shop, she put
All her best things in one long narrow room.
The place smelt old, of things too long kept shut,
The smell of absences where shadows come
That can't be polished. There was nothing then
To give her own reflection back again.

And when she died I felt no grief at all,
Only the guilt of what I once refused.
I walked into her room among the tall
Sideboards and cupboards – things she never used
But needed: and no finger-marks were there,
Only the new dust falling through the air.

PASSAGE FROM CHILDHOOD

Where hell was open and the threshold crossed,
With seven deadly torments in my head
I walked and lived. At dark, wide-eyed I tossed
Feeling my body feverish on the bed
Certain I was among the chosen lost.

Each impulse paused before me, not my own
But rather like a rag flung in my face,
And wishes to apologise, atone,
Feel eight years' wickedness wrapped up in grace –
The terror, yet the need to be alone.

Looked back at now, the fires of hell retreat
Yet the responsibilities still feel
Like breath blown at me from that furious heat.
I move beyond the gestures of my will,
Careful of each handshake, of each heartbeat.

But now I know that all the agony
Built a compassion that I need to share.
The torment of that childhood teaches me
That when I listen now or simply stare
Fears are exchanged and exorcized – and free.

IN PRAISE OF CREATION

That one bird, one star,
The one flash of the tiger's eye
Purely assert what they are,
Without ceremony testify.

Testify to order, to rule –
How the birds mate at one time only,
How the sky is, for a certain time, full
Of birds, the moon sometimes cut thinly.

And the tiger trapped in the cage of his skin,
Watchful over creation, rests
For the blood to pound, the drums to begin,
Till the tigress' shadow casts

A darkness over him, a passion, a scent,
The world goes turning, turning, the season
Sieves earth to its one sure element
And the blood beats beyond reason.

Then quiet, and birds folding their wings,
The new moon waiting for years to be stared at here,
The season sinks to satisfied things –
Man with his mind ajar.

WORLD I HAVE NOT MADE

I have sometimes thought how it would have been
if I had had to create the whole thing myself –
my life certainly but also something else;
I mean a world which I could inhabit freely,
ideas, objects, everything prepared;
not ideas simply as Plato knew them,
shadows of shadows, but more like furniture,
something to move around and live in,
something *I* had made. But still there would be
all that I hadn't made – animals, stars,
tides tugging against me, moon uncaring,
and the trying to love without reciprocity.
All this is here still. It is hard, hard,
even with free faith outlooking boundaries,
to come to terms with obvious suffering.
I live in a world I have not created
inward or outward. There is a sweetness
in willing surrender: I trail my ideas
behind great truths. My ideas are like shadows
and sometimes I consider how it would have been
to create a credo, objects, ideas
and then to live with them. I can understand
when tides most tug and the moon is remote
and the trapped wild beast is one with its shadow,
how even great faith leaves room for abysses
and the taut mind turns to its own requirings.

(19)

HARVEST AND CONSECRATION

After the heaped piles and the cornsheaves waiting
To be collected, gathered into barns,
After all fruits have burst their skins, the sating
    Season cools and turns,
And then I think of something that you said
Of when you held the chalice and the bread.

I spoke of Mass and thought of it as close
To how a season feels which stirs and brings
Fire to the hearth, food to the hungry house
    And strange, uncovered things –
God in a garden then in sheaves of corn
And the white bread a way to be reborn.

I thought of priest as midwife and as mother
Feeling the pain, feeling the pleasure too,
    All opposites together,
Until you said no one could feel such passion
And still preserve the power of consecration.

And it is true. How cool the gold sheaves lie,
Rich without need to ask for any more
Richness. The seed, the simple thing must die
    If only to restore
Our faith in fruitful, hidden things. I see
The wine and bread protect our ecstasy.

A WORLD OF LIGHT

Yes when the dark withdrew I suffered light
And saw the candles heave beneath their wax,
I watched the shadow of my old self dwindle
As softly on my recollection stole
A mood the senses could not touch or damage,
A sense of peace beyond the breathing word.

Day dawdled at my elbow. It was night
Within. I saw my hands, their soft dark backs
Keeping me from the noise outside. The candle
Seemed snuffed into a deep and silent pool:
It drew no shadow round my constant image
For in a dazzling dark my spirit stirred.

But still I questioned it. My inward sight
Still knew the senses and the senses' tracks,
I felt my flesh and clothes, a rubbing sandal,
And distant voices wishing to console.
My mind was keen to understand and rummage
To find assurance in the sounds I heard.

Then senses ceased and thoughts were driven quite
Away (no act of mine). I could relax
And feel a fire no earnest prayer can kindle;
Old parts of peace dissolved into a whole
And like a bright thing proud in its new plumage
My mind was keen as an attentive bird.

Yes, fire, light, air, birds, wax, the sun's own height
I draw from now, but every image breaks.
Only a child's simplicity can handle
Such moments when the hottest fire feels cool,
And every breath is like a sudden homage
To peace that penetrates and is not feared.

NOTES FOR A BOOK OF HOURS

I

Kneeling to pray and resting on the words
I feel a stillness that I have not made.
Shadows take root, the falling light is laid
Smoothly on stone and skin. I lean towards
Some meaning that's delayed.

It is as if the mind had nervous fingers,
Could touch and apprehend yet not possess.
The light is buried where the darkness lingers
And something grateful in me wants to bless
Simply from happiness.

The world dreams through me in this sudden spring.
My senses itch although the stillness stays.
God is too large a word for me to sing,
Some touch upon my spirit strums and plays:
What images will bring

This moment down to words that I can use
When not so rapt? The hours, the hours increase.
All is a movement, shadows now confuse,
Darkening the soft wings of the doves of peace,
And can I tame or choose?

II

I have to start the whole thing from the source,
Go back behind the noisy tower of tongues,
Press on my words new meanings, make my songs
Like breath from uncontaminated lungs
Or water from a new-found water-course.

Not to convince you, that is not my aim,
Simply to speak and to be gladly heard.
I have the oils, the waters, but the name
Eludes me still. Within a single word
I want the christening, the flowering flame.

Men had it once who carved far out of sight
Demons and angels, all anonymous;
Skill was another name for pure delight.
My angels must convince, be obvious.
I must create the substance and the light.

The cosmic vision fades. Within my mind
The images are laid, books on a shelf
Dusty and old. I only need to find
Some way to show the struggle in myself –
The demons watchful but the angels blind.

III

In the cool cloisters and the choirs I hear
The open-handed words, the pleading psalms.
The chant is sober and it soothes and calms
Though what the words depict is full of fear;
I gather all the shadows in my arms.

I cannot sing but only hear and trace
The meaning underneath the echoes, wait
For the resumption of a scattered state.
Such concentration screwed into my face –
Can it reflect an inner mood of grace?

What do they think who kneel within those stalls,
Young, old, white, black? The world outside still gropes
Not for a paradise but for its hopes
Come true in time. The chanting sinks and falls –
The great bell silent, none to pull the ropes.

IV

The sound is ordered, cool.
I heard somebody say
Once that the liturgy is diffused
Theology. I think they meant the way
The music and the words are used,
Austere yet beautiful.

A world of dogma can
Within these hours be pressed.
Both day and night are counted by
The times of exhortation and of rest.
The psalms can both rejoice and sigh,
Serve every need of man.

I need to make my own
Great book of hours, record
Matins and lauds, prime, terce and vespers,
With no authority but my own word.
The psalms are loud with truth; in whispers
I mark my hours alone.

A CONFESSION

It seemed the most unlikely place to bring
One's childhood back. Outside, the grown world clung
To light, or did the light engender it?
Within the church, all that was old revived –
Gold on the roof, and in the shining apse
Mosaics stood within a lively stillness.
All was perpetual and precious here.

And here a foreigner, though recognised
By gentleness that leaps ahead of language,
I could discourse of every shameful topic,
Reveal the secret passions of a childhood,
Speak, fumblingly, the fears of adolescence.
And still the gold mosaics went on shining
And still, outside, the city played with light.

Exiles, perhaps, are people without shadows,
Movers beyond the sequences of time.
Simply to speak here is to be accepted.
Or does the light play tricks with one's own past,
Show it unshameful? Does one here mark time
Not with the stamping foot's impatient beat
But with surrender, attribute of love?

A REQUIEM

It is the ritual not the fact
That brings a held emotion to
Its breaking-point. This man I knew
Only a little, by his death
Shows me a love I thought I lacked
And all the stirrings underneath.

It is the calm, the solemn thing,
Not the distracted mourners cry
Or the cold place where dead things lie,
That teaches me I cannot claim
To stand aside. These tears which sting –
Are they from sorrow or from shame?

AT A MASS

Waiting restlessly the coming event,
Hearing the three bells ringing the loud warning,
I look for the lifted moment, the lifted cup,
Feeling upon my skin the Roman morning.
I watch with a critical eye the bread raised up
And confuse aesthetics now with a sacrament.

It is the veils drawn over, the decent hiding
That recall the decorum the test of art demands.
Around me the people pray, forgetful of
Even their painful eyes, their well-worn hands.
I struggle now with my own ideas of love
And wonder if art and religion mean dividing.

Each has his way and mine perhaps is to
Suffer the critical sense that cannot rest.
If the air is cool, the colours right, the spoken
Words dramatic enough, then I am pleased.
But why must I ask a sense of style in the broken
Bread and bring God down to my limited view?

Pride enfolds me, pride in the gift of tongues;
Envy too, since I long to be like these
Who approach with empty hands, an open heart –
The simple men lost in simplicities.
I have to endure the ecstatic pain of art
And shape from the silence all my encroaching songs.

Emptiness, space. Darkness you could put walls round, set stars in, light from far off but never unthinkingly enter. To approach was to become the darkness, not even assisted by shadows.

And the senses, too, disarmed, discouraged, withdrawn by choice from pleasure. Finger not touching, crushing cool leaves. Lips closed against mouth or assuagement. Ears un-entered by voices. Hands held out but empty. Even the darkness could not be possessed.

All indescribable then, but still the urge to depict, descry, point out, picture, prepare. The deep darkness had to be spoken of, touched beyond reach of stars, entered without indications.

Flame, then, firm – not the inward flame of passion, urgent, wanting appeasement, close to the senses and sighing through them: but a pure light pouring through windows, flooding the glass but leaving the glass unaltered.

More than this too. Not light limited by tapers, drawn to its strength by the darkness around it, not puffed out by wind or increased by careful breath.

It is held in being by patience, by watching, suffering beyond signs or words. Not your light either. You are receiver, requirer. And when the flame falters nothing of yours can revive it: you are resigned to the darkness. And you open your eyes to the world.

Bridges. Ways over and ways to wait. Place for a stance or a stillness. Places, too, for violence. Bridges are blown and a war starts.

And in the water you can see the fish – if you watch carefully, if you side-step your own shadow, if you gaze deeper than self-love or arrogance.

Many have paused here. Have noted the faint sky reflected, the full moon falling, it seems, in the water. Have fallen in love with the dark.

For her, they were ways merely. Bridges meant building, meant the creak of planks, the delicate balance where wood is articulate, where men move as one, where the water is conquered.

Where prayer is most painful, she sought for an image. Others learnt light, air, steps, birds (the dove as a pretext or omen). All insubstantial for her. She needed the passion, the building, something to cleave – and connect.

Not standing there, letting the night drown in the water, watching the dear shadows that hold off the mountain. For her, the poise before the moment's abandon, all the reprisals of pain.

Pope, people, kings, confessors came to her. Proud professions passed over her bridges. Only Siena – round hill-city, seething with feud and friendship – was the safe place, solid ground, sweet summit where winds meet. Only here were bridges redundant.

Can light heal? Can the fountain surrender? Dare the fisherman pause? Her bridges were built for a journey. The unconcerned waters flowed on.

THE RESURRECTION

I was the one who waited in the garden
Doubting the morning and the early light.
I watched the mist lift off its own soft burden,
Permitting not believing my own sight.

If there were sudden noises I dismissed
Them as a trick of sound, a sleight of hand.
Not by a natural joy could I be blessed
Or trust a thing I could not understand.

Maybe I was a shadow thrown by one
Who, weeping, came to lift away the stone,
Or was I but the path on which the sun,
Too heavy for itself, was loosed and thrown?

I heard the voices and the recognition
And love like kisses heard behind thin walls.
Were they my tears which fell, a real contrition?
Or simply April with its waterfalls?

It was by negatives I learnt my place.
The garden went on growing and I sensed
A sudden breeze that blew across my face.
Despair returned but now it danced, it danced.

THE COUNTERPART

Since clarity suggests simplicity
And since the simple thing is here inapt,
    I choose obscurities of tongue and touch,
The shadow side of language and the dark
    Hinted in conversations close to quarrel,
Conceived within the mind in aftermaths.
    The intellect no crystal is but swarming
Darkness on darkness, gently ruffled by
    The senses as they draw an image home.

    If art must be abstract that needs to speak
In honesty, in painful honesty,
    Then every scene must be composed likewise,
Familiar objects turn to careful shapes,
    Gestures be stiff, emotions emblematic.
So art makes peace with honesty and we
    Detect a blazing, a Byzantine world,
A formal image shining from the dark
    But no less enigmatic than the dark.

    Only in such decorum can our pain
Survive without dilution or pretence.
    The agony of loss, the potent thrust
Of seed that never will become a child
    Need the severity of metaphor,
The symbol on the shield, the dove, the lion
    Fixed in a stillness where the darkness folds
In pleated curtains, nothing disarranged:
    And only then the eye begins to see.

MANTEGNA'S *AGONY IN THE GARDEN*

The agony is formal; three
Bodies are stretched in pure repose,
One's halo leans against a tree,
Over a book his fingers close:
One's arms are folded carefully.

The third man lies with sandalled feet
Thrust in the path. They almost touch
Three playful rabbits. Down the street,
Judas and his procession march
Making the distance seem discreet.

Even the praying figure has
A cared-for attitude. This art
Puts down the city and the mass
Of mountains like a counterpart
Of pain disguised as gentleness.

And yet such careful placing here
Of mountain, men and agony,
Being so solid makes more clear
The pain. Pain is particular.
The foreground shows a barren tree:
Is it a vulture crouching there,
No symbol but a prophecy?

THE RETREAT

Here in this room, the very top of the tower,
I live a little. On these checkered walls
Some past is written and some ancient power
Is whispered in those finger-marks and scrawls –
Childhood or family history or war?
Or were the things inventions, always false?

One window, steep enough to hold the sky,
Holds the sea too; today the water's calm,
The cumbered breakers have smoothed out and lie
As if no ripple cut across their firm
And balanced movement. Meanwhile, slowly I
Sit meditating, head upon my arm.

Silence is spread for me and no one knows
That I am here; no one can point and say
'Escaper both from failure and applause.'
The tongues of fire have not come down today
Nor the descending doves of peace. I close
My door and make my peace in my own way.

And shall be better when I climb the stairs
Downward to darkness and the still-calm sea.
Voices will snatch me and the old despairs
Return. One moment, recollectedly
I understand old silences and prayers
Yet know that something else is meant for me.

VISIT TO AN ARTIST

FOR DAVID JONES

Window upon the wall, a balcony
With a light chair, the air and water so
Mingled you could not say which was the sun
And which the adamant yet tranquil spray.
But nothing was confused and nothing slow:
Each way you looked always the sea, the sea.

And every shyness that we brought with us
Was drawn into the pictures on the walls.
It was so good to sit quite still and lose
Necessity of discourse, words to choose
And wonder which were honest and which false.

Then I remembered words that you had said
Of art as gesture and as sacrament,
A mountain under the calm form of paint
Much like the Presence under wine and bread –
Art with its largesse and its own restraint.

THE CLOWN

I

Balloon on finger he watches us, the clown;
White cheeks conceal what eyes are witness of
And nimble body hides in pantaloon.
If you love this it is yourself you love,
Your own absurdity, your pride brought down.

But is this what he means, or does he mean
A dancing childish world where play is fact?
The rubber ball returns unburst and clean –
Your world so shapely, blown up but intact?
Are *you* the dancer in a pasteboard scene.

I am afraid of things which can be hurt.
The clown as much as cringing animals
Invites my wounding. Yet my pain will start
Because I wound. The clown prevails in art;
Gently as his balloon, my pity falls.

THE CLOWN

II

Aloof, reserved, yet strangely vulnerable,
Making of art a nonchalance, mere skill

As though a skill were something not to care
Too much about. You throw balls in the air,

You make yourself ridiculous, your face
Fitting nowhere but in a taut white space.

Yet sometimes carelessly you have been drawn
By painters in their note-book moments when

A special grace appears but fits nowhere –
A harlequin who leans upon a chair,

A youth who idly strums an old guitar,
Each lazy gesture meaning 'I don't care.'

THE CLOWN

III

Others are noble and admired –
The ones who walk the tightrope without nets,
The one who goes inside the lion's cage,
And all the grave, audacious acrobats.
Away from fear and rage
He simply is the interval for tired

People who cannot bear
Too much excitement. They can see in him
Their own lost innocence or else their fear
(For him no metal bars or broken limb).
Have they forgotten that it takes as much
Boldness to tumble, entertain and jest
When loneliness walks tightropes in your breast
And every joke is like a wild beast's touch?

THE CLOWN

IV

If I painted you
It would not be as juggler or as one who
Played the fool and entertained the crowds.
I would have you entirely alone,
Thoughtful and leaning
Against a dark window that needed cleaning.

I would want to show you
Not as victim or scapegoat,
Not like one who is hurried away, loaded
With other people's fears, goaded
Into the distance, but rather
As one who uses distance as a tether,
Tied but detached,
Sympathetic yet remote.

Strangely you remind
Of Christ on the cross.
Is it the seeming surrender or the white face,
The acceptance of loss?
Or simply that you seem like one not fallen from grace,
Innocent through knowledge,
Assenting yet resigned?

THE CLOWN

V

The eager one unconscious of himself,
Drawing the bow across the strings, absorbed
In music or the version that he makes,

The smiling one who never seems afraid,
Something to offer always yet not hoarding
His own or others' thoughts of what he is –

Simply the one who does not analyse
But still can gauge the feelings that surround him,
Loosen the taut voice, spread the narrow smile.

My childhood stands abruptly at my elbow
Forbidding demonstration, looking in,
Seeing the wishes and the dancers there.

THE CLOWN

VI

Something he has to say
Concerning pain. You have to watch the dance
With utmost concentration, in the way
A child will watch until the view enchants
And he is lost in it. The clown is gay
    And terrible at once.

His face will never show
You any hint of what you ought to feel:
White greasepaint spreads across his cheeks like snow.
His jokes seem feeble and his tricks are slow,
    He seems a game, unreal.

And yet his helplessness,
His lack of tragic gesture, tragic mood,
Remind me of the abject beast we press
Our own despairs on, Christ nailed to the wood.
There are more ways to make a wilderness
    Than we have understood.

LAZARUS

It was the amazing white, it was the way he simply
Refused to answer our questions, it was the cold pale glance
Of death upon him, the smell of death that truly
Declared his rising to us. It was no chance
Happening, as a man may fill a silence
Between two heart-beats, seem to be dead and then
Astonish us with the closeness of his presence;
This man was dead, I say it again and again.
All of our sweating bodies moved towards him
And our minds moved too, hungry for finished faith.
He would not enter our world at once with words
That we might be tempted to twist or argue with:
Cold like a white root pressed in the bowels of earth
He looked, but also vulnerable – like birth.

THE DIAMOND CUTTER

Not what the light will do but how he shapes it
And what particular colours it will bear,

And something of the climber's concentration
Seeing the white peak, setting the right foot there.

Not how the sun was plausible at morning
Nor how it was distributed at noon,

And not how much the single stone could show
But rather how much brilliance it would shun;

Simply a paring down, a cleaving to
One object, as the star-gazer who sees

One single comet polished by its fall
Rather than countless, untouched galaxies.

STARGAZERS AND OTHERS

One, staring out stars,
Lost himself in looking and almost
Forgot glass, eye, air, space;
Simply, he thought, the world is improved
By my staring, how the still glass leaps
When the sky thuds in like tides.

Another, making love, once
Stared so far over his pleasure
That woman, world, the spiral
Of taut bodies, the clinging hands, broke apart
And he saw, as the stargazer sees,
Landscapes made to be looked at,
Fruit to fall, not be plucked.

In you also something
Of such vision occurs.
How else would I have learnt
The tapered stars, the pause
On the nervous spiral? Names I need
Stronger than love, desire,
Passion, pleasure. Oh discover
Some star and christen it, but let me be
The space that your eye moves over.

TO A FRIEND WITH A RELIGIOUS VOCATION

FOR C.

Thinking of your vocation, I am filled
With thoughts of my own lack of one. I see
Within myself no wish to breed or build
Or take the three vows ringed by poverty.
     And yet I have a sense,
Vague and inchoate, with no symmetry,
Of purpose. Is it merely a pretence,

A kind of scaffolding which I erect
Half out of fear, half out of laziness?
The fitful poems come but can't protect
The empty areas of loneliness.
     You know what you must do,
So that mere breathing is a way to bless.
Dark nights, perhaps, but no grey days for you.

Your vows enfold you. I must make my own;
Now this, now that, each one empirical.
My poems move from feelings not yet known,
And when the poem is written I can feel
     A flash, a moment's peace.
The curtain will be drawn across your grille.
My silences are always enemies.

Yet with the same convictions that you have
(It is but your vocation that I lack),
I must, like you, believe in perfect love.
It is the dark, the dark that draws me back
    Into a chaos where
Vocations, visions fail, the will grows slack
And I am stunned by silence everywhere.

CHILDREN AND DEATH

Not to be spoken of, they will not let
    Us enter rooms where anyone has died,
And they put candles by our beds, a light
    That keeps us watchful and more terrified

Than any dear familiar darkness where
    Our shadows slip away. We dream of death
Sweet and apparent in the freedom there
    And ape a dying by a withheld breath.

Nor do they know our games have room enough
    For death and sickness. We have stretched them out
Further than childhood or parents' love
    And further even than the breath of doubt.

A KIND OF UNDERSTANDING

You could say anything; she'd listen
Sitting in the corner (a bundle of fur
With cobwebs for string, somebody called her),
Deep in her sewing. Her eyes seemed to glisten
With help and encouragement. Yes, you could stir

And never be punished, always could say
Just what you thought. She seemed beyond shock
Or fear. There was something about the way
She held her sewing, like a child to rock:
She would not drop stitches or let edges fray.

A complete world – yet with a door
For anyone's entrance. An old midwife
Ready for birth or death, to restore
Things to their places. If it was life
She could cut cords: if death, she'd prepare
Fresh flowers and sympathy. Each knew the knife.

Sometimes you'd find her holding her beads,
Begging for silence, gesturing you
To sit down and wait. Always she knew
Time for the harvest and place for the seeds,
Having no words for the things that she grew
Yet, like an instinct, fulfilling all needs.

VISIT TO A FRIEND IN HOSPITAL

Always I was afraid of hospitals,
The green, inhuman, quiet corridors,
The dark impersonal numbers on the doors;
No echo could exist along those walls.
Death would be easy there and quite expected –
A sigh, a silence, and a room rejected.

Thus nursing-homes and hospitals appeared
To me, a child. Now when I visit you
I have to live the older horror through –
The smells, the dry heat, and the voices heard
Low and discreet. I fight away the fear
That death may stand behind each quiet door.

You are the one to whom I bring distress,
The troubles, dreams and all the broken things.
The rôles reverse and I'm the one who brings
Solicitude and help and tenderness.
And yet it is a mask I wear, an act
Where terror hides behind the look of tact.

I walk upright and strong, yet I am weak,
While you who lie in pain have all the power.
I come to call at the appointed hour
Like one who long ago had learnt to seek,
Through sickness, darkness, death, a hem to touch.
The cure was granted. Do I ask too much?

GREEK STATUES

These I have never touched but only looked at.
If you could say that stillness meant surrender
These are surrendered.
Yet their large audacious gestures signify surely
Remonstrance, reprisal? What have they left to lose
But the crumbling away by rain or time? Defiance
For them is a dignity, a declaration.

Odd how one wants to touch not simply stare,
To run one's fingers over the flanks and arms,
Not to possess, rather to be possessed.
Bronze is bright to the eye but under the hands
Is cool and calming. Gods into silent metal:

To stone also, not to the palpable flesh.
Incarnations are elsewhere and more human,
Something concerning us; but these are other.
It is as if something infinite, remote
Permitted intrusion. It is as if these blind eyes
Exposed a landscape precious with grapes and olives:
And our probing hands move not to grasp but praise.

THE PRIDE OF LIFE: A ROMAN SETTING

Old men discourse upon wise topics here:
Children and women pass the shadows by,
    Only the young are desperate. Their clear
And unambiguous gazes strike
    Against each brushing hand or eye,
        Their faces like

O something far away, maybe a cave
Where looks and actions always moved to hunt,
    Where every gesture knew how to behave
And there was never space between
    The easy having and the want.
        I think the keen

Primitive stares that pierce this decorous street
Look to some far back mood and time to claim
    A life beyond the urbane and effete
Where youth from coolest childhood came,
    And look to look was like the hunter's throw –
    Perpetually new and long ago.

MEN FISHING IN THE ARNO

I do not know what they are catching,
I only know that they stand there, leaning
A little like lovers, eager but not demanding,
Waiting and hoping for a catch, money,
A meal tomorrow but today, still there, steady.

And the river also moves as calmly
From the waterfall slipping to a place
A mind could match its thought with.
And above, the cypresses with cool gestures
Command the city, give it formality.

It is like this every day but more especially
On Sundays; every few yards you see a fisherman,
Each independent, none
Working with others and yet accepting
Others. From this one might, I think,

Build a whole way of living – men in their mazes
Of secret desires yet keeping a sense
Of order outwardly, hoping
Not too flamboyantly, satisfied with little
Yet not surprised should the river suddenly
Yield a hundredfold, every hunger appeased.

AN ENGLISH SUMMER

An English summer – and a sense of form
Rides the five senses that dispute their claims.
Lawns levelled against nature, airs which warm
Each plant, perpetuate the hours and names.
We cannot see beyond the blue; no storm
Vies with the children ardent at their games.

Childhood returns with summer. It is strange
That such a season brings one's memories back.
Springs have their homesickness, autumns arrange
The sweet nostalgias that we long to lack.
But summer is itself; it's we who change
And lay our childhoods on the golden stack.

My fingers rest and eyes concern their sight
Simply with what would live were I not here.
It is the concentration of the light
That shows the other side of pain and fear.
I watch, incredulous of such delight,
Wanting the meaning not the landscape clear.

Was it for this the breath once breathed upon
The waters that we rose from? I can see
Only a summer with its shadows gone,
Skies that refuse an alien dignity.
But gardens, gardens echo. What sun shone
To make this truce with pain and ecstasy?

THE ROOM

This room I know so well becomes
A way to keep proportion near.
In other houses, other rooms
Only anomalies appear.

I chose these books, the pictures too,
Thinking that I would often look
Upon a canvas like a view
Or find a world within a book.

They lie or hang, each laden now
With my own past, yet there's no sign
For anyone who does not know
Me, that these attributes are mine.

Strange paradox – that I collect
Objects to liberate myself.
This room so heavy now, so decked
Has put my past upon a shelf.

And this is freedom – not to need
To choose those things again. I thus
Preside upon the present, cede
The ornaments to usefulness.

And yet I know that while I clear
The ground and win back liberty,
Tomorrow's debris settles here
To make my art, to alter me.

TWO DEATHS

It was only a film,
Perhaps I shall say later
Forgetting the story, left only
With bright images – the blazing dawn
Over the European ravaged pain,
And a white unsaddled horse, the only calm
Living creature. Will only such pictures remain?

Or shall I see
The shot boy running, running
Clutching the white sheet on the washing-line,
Looking at his own blood like a child
Who never saw blood before and feels defiled,
A boy dying without dignity
Yet brave still, trying to stop himself from falling
And screaming – his white girl waiting just out of calling?

I am ashamed
Not to have seen anyone dead,
Anyone I know I mean;
Odd that yesterday also
I saw a broken cat stretched on a path,
Not quite finished. Its gentle head
Showed one eye staring, mutely beseeching
Death, it seemed. All day
I have thought of death, of violence and death,
Of the blazing Polish light, of the cat's eye:
I am ashamed I have never seen anyone die.

ABOUT THESE THINGS

About these things I always shall be dumb.
Some wear their silences as more than dress,
As more than skin-deep. I bear mine like some

Scar that is hidden out of shamefulness.
I speak from depths I do not understand
Yet cannot find the words for this distress.

So much of power is put into my hand
When words come easily. I sense the way
People are charmed and pause; I seem to mend

Some hurt. Some healing seems to make them stay.
And yet within the power that I use
My wordless fears remain. Perhaps I say

In lucid verse the terrors that confuse
In conversation. Maybe I am dumb
Because if fears were spoken I would lose

The lovely languages I do not choose
More than the darknesses from which they come.

NO REPLY

Between acceptance and the sense of loss
I pause, reluctant to admit the blame.
Leaves lie along the streets as if to gloss
A grief they never knew, could never name.
I watch them, knowing I am still the same.

Love has its battles and its counterparts
But friendship has to make rules of its own
Both for betrayals and for broken hearts,
Also for feelings that were never shown;
Emotion's not explained by thought alone.

Love could be stressed in touches and in looks.
We only have the easy words we say
When close together. Words seem out of books
When there is any absence or delay;
Distances not our selves, perhaps, betray.

My letters go, hectic with crossings-out,
Having no substitute for pause in speech.
I wait for answers, building out of doubt
More feeling than mere friendships ever reach,
Learning a lesson I would fear to teach.

THE UNFULFILLED

It was love only that we knew
At first. We did not dispossess
Each other of the total view
That is quite blurred when passions pass.
I felt myself, acknowledged you.

When did desire enter and
Confuse the sweetness, heat the blood?
On meeting we could understand,
Wordless, each other's every mood.
Where does love start and friendship end?

Impediments have set apart
The impulse from fruition. We,
Who have no compass but the heart,
Must learn an immaturity,
Though all the later passions hurt.

By acts of will we now must find
Each other as we were at first,
Unthwarted then and unconfined.
Yes, but I have an aching thirst
That can't be quenched by a cool mind.

We must stand side by side and live
As if the past were still to come.
It is our needs we need to give
And fashion from their anguish some
Love that has no wish to deceive
But rests contented, being dumb.

(60)

NO CHILD

We touch and when our hands
Meet, a world rises up,
A hemisphere extends,
Rivers we cannot stop.
Yet something is withheld –
No marriage and no child.

Our fields that seem so thick
With corn, that make an edge
Of gold, play us a trick;
It is a barren hedge,
A stony, sterile field:
No marriage and no child.

Yet barrenness also
Is tender. Others give
To children what we show
Each other. We can live
Sufficiently fulfilled,
No marriage and no child.

And what a child might take
In flesh and blood and mind
To the edge of heartbreak,
We hand over and find
That each of us can build
Out of this love, a child.

THE INSTRUMENT

Only in our imaginations
The act is done, for you have spoken
Vows that can never now be broken.
I keep them too – with reservations;
Yet acts not done can still be taken
Away, like all completed passions.

But what can not be taken is
Satiety. Cool space lies near
Our bodies – a parenthesis
Between a pleasure and a fear.
Our loving is composed of this
Touching of strings to make sounds clear.

A touching, then a glancing off.
It is your vows that stretch between
Us like an instrument of love
Where only echoes intervene.
Yet these exchanges are enough
Since strings touched only are most keen.

REMEMBERING FIREWORKS

Always as if for the first time we watch
The fireworks as if no one had ever
Done this before, made shapes, signs,
Cut diamonds on air, sent up stars
Nameless, imperious. And in the falling
Of fire, the spent rocket, there is a kind
Of nostalgia as normally only attaches
To things long known and lost. Such an absence,
Such emptiness of sky the fireworks leave
After their festival. We, fumbling
For words of love, remember the rockets,
The spinning wheels, the sudden diamonds,
And say with delight 'Yes, like that, like that.'
Oh and the air is full of falling
Stars surrendered. We search for a sign.